AI for Accountants: The Complete Guide to Mastering Artificial Intelligence in Finance

by Bob Halley

AI for Accountants: The Complete Guide to Mastering Artificial Intelligence in Finance

Mastering Artificial Intelligence in Modern Accounting

By Bob Halley

Table of Contents

12. The Future of AI in Accounting

Chapter 1: Introduction to AI in Accounting

Introduction to AI in Accounting

The accounting profession is undergoing a profound transformation, driven by rapid advancements in artificial intelligence (AI). What was once a field dominated by manual data entry and spreadsheet analysis is now evolving into a dynamic, tech-enabled discipline where AI tools are reshaping workflows, improving accuracy, and unlocking new opportunities for strategic decision-making. For accountants, understanding AI is no longer optional—it's essential to staying competitive in a rapidly changing industry. This chapter introduces the fundamental concepts of AI, explains why it matters for accountants, and explores the practical applications that are revolutionizing the profession. By the end of this chapter, you'll have a clear understanding of AI's potential and how to begin leveraging it in your work.

What is AI? Demystifying Artificial Intelligence

Artificial intelligence (AI) refers to the ability of machines to perform tasks that typically require human intelligence, such as learning, reasoning, and problem-solving. While this may sound complex, the core technologies behind AI are designed to simplify and enhance everyday tasks. For accountants, AI tools are not about replacing human expertise but about augmenting it, allowing professionals to focus on higher-value activities.

At the heart of AI are several key technologies. Machine learning (ML) enables systems to learn from data and improve over time without explicit programming. For example, an AI-powered tool might analyze patterns in financial transactions to identify anomalies or predict future trends. Natural language processing (NLP) allows machines to understand and generate human language, making it possible for chatbots to answer client queries or for software to extract relevant information from unstructured documents. Robotic process automation (RPA) automates repetitive tasks, such as data entry or invoice processing, freeing up valuable time for accountants to focus on strategic analysis.

One common misconception about AI is that it will replace accountants entirely. In reality, AI is a tool that enhances human capabilities. For instance, AI-powered software can automate routine tasks like reconciling accounts or categorizing expenses, but it still requires human oversight to interpret results and make strategic decisions. By understanding these technologies, accountants can better appreciate how AI can support their work rather than fearing it as a threat.

Why AI Matters for Accountants

The accounting profession is no stranger to technological change. From the introduction of spreadsheets to cloud-based accounting software, technology has continually reshaped how accountants work. AI represents the next wave of innovation, offering solutions to some of the industry's most pressing challenges.

One of the biggest pain points for accountants is manual data entry. Not only is this time-consuming, but it's also prone to errors. AI tools can automate these tasks, reducing errors and freeing up time for more strategic work. Similarly, compliance is becoming increasingly complex, with ever-changing regulations and the need for accurate reporting. AI can help by analyzing vast amounts of data to ensure compliance and flagging potential issues before they become problems.

Another key benefit of AI is its ability to handle the growing complexity of financial data. With businesses generating more data than ever before, traditional methods of analysis are no longer sufficient. AI can process large datasets quickly, uncovering insights that would be difficult or impossible to detect manually. For example, predictive analytics can help accountants forecast future financial trends, enabling better decision-making for their clients or organizations.

AI adoption in accounting is on the rise, with many leading firms already leveraging these tools to gain a competitive edge. According to recent industry reports, over 50% of accounting firms are investing in AI to improve efficiency and accuracy. For accountants, embracing AI isn't just about keeping up with the times—it's about staying ahead in a competitive landscape.

Overview of AI Applications in Accounting

AI is transforming accounting in numerous ways, from automating repetitive tasks to providing advanced analytics. Here are some of the most impactful applications:

Automation of Repetitive Tasks: Tools like RPA can handle tasks such as invoice processing, bank reconciliations, and payroll management. For example, an AI-powered system might automatically match invoices to purchase orders and flag discrepancies, reducing the need for manual intervention.

Predictive Analytics: Machine learning algorithms can analyze historical data to forecast future trends, such as cash flow or revenue growth. This enables accountants to provide proactive advice to clients or make informed decisions for their organizations.

Fraud Detection: AI can identify unusual patterns in financial data that may indicate fraud. For instance, an anomaly detection algorithm might flag transactions that deviate from typical behavior, allowing accountants to investigate potential issues early.

Tax Compliance: AI-powered tools can streamline tax preparation by automatically identifying deductions, ensuring compliance with regulations, and flagging potential audit risks. This reduces the burden on accountants and minimizes errors.

Financial Forecasting: By analyzing market trends and historical data, AI can help accountants predict future financial performance, enabling better planning and resource allocation.

These applications are already delivering measurable results for businesses. For example, a mid-sized accounting firm reduced errors by 30% and cut processing time in half by implementing AI-powered automation tools. Similarly, a multinational corporation improved fraud detection accuracy by 40% using machine learning algorithms.

Getting Started with AI in Accounting

For accountants new to AI, the first step is identifying low-risk opportunities to integrate AI into your workflows. Start by pinpointing repetitive tasks that could be automated, such as data entry or report generation. These are ideal candidates for AI adoption because they offer immediate efficiency gains without requiring a complete overhaul of your processes.

Next, evaluate AI tools and vendors to find solutions that align with your needs. Look for reputable providers with a track record of success in the accounting industry. Many vendors offer free trials or demos, allowing you to test the software before committing.

Building foundational knowledge is also crucial. Consider pursuing training or certifications in AI to better understand its capabilities and limitations. Many professional organizations offer courses tailored to accountants, covering topics such as machine learning, NLP, and RPA.

It's important to approach AI adoption with a balanced perspective. While AI can enhance efficiency and accuracy, it's not a substitute for human judgment. Accountants must maintain oversight to ensure that AI-generated insights are accurate and relevant. Over-reliance on AI without proper oversight can lead to errors or missed opportunities.

Case Studies: AI Success Stories in Accounting

Real-world examples illustrate the transformative potential of AI in accounting. One notable case is a mid-sized accounting firm that implemented AI-powered automation tools to streamline its workflows. By automating routine tasks like invoice processing and bank reconciliations, the firm reduced errors by 30% and cut processing time in half. This allowed accountants to focus on higher-value activities, such as financial planning and advisory services.

Another success story comes from a multinational corporation that leveraged machine learning algorithms to improve fraud detection. By analyzing patterns in financial transactions, the AI system identified anomalies that indicated potential fraud. As a result, the company improved fraud detection accuracy by 40%, saving millions of dollars in potential losses.

These case studies highlight best practices for AI adoption, such as starting with low-risk applications, selecting the right tools, and maintaining human oversight. They also demonstrate the tangible benefits of AI, from increased efficiency to improved accuracy and decision-making.

The Future of AI in Accounting

The future of AI in accounting is full of potential. Emerging technologies like generative AI—which can create new content, such as financial reports or tax documents—are poised to further revolutionize the profession. AI is also playing a growing role in sustainability reporting, helping businesses track and analyze their environmental impact. Additionally, AI has the potential to democratize financial insights, making advanced analytics accessible to small businesses that may not have the resources for traditional consulting services.

As AI continues to evolve, accountants must embrace it as a strategic imperative. Those who invest in understanding and leveraging AI will be better equipped to thrive in a rapidly changing landscape. Whether it's automating routine tasks, uncovering hidden insights, or providing proactive advice, AI offers countless opportunities to enhance the value accountants bring to their clients and organizations.

AI is transforming the accounting profession in profound ways, offering solutions to longstanding challenges and unlocking new opportunities for growth. By automating repetitive tasks, providing advanced analytics, and enhancing decision-making, AI empowers accountants to focus on strategic, high-value activities. The key to success lies in understanding AI's capabilities, identifying opportunities for integration, and maintaining a balanced approach that combines technology with human expertise.

As we look to the future, one thing is clear: AI is not just a tool for accountants—it's a strategic partner that can help them thrive in an increasingly complex and competitive industry. By embracing AI, accountants can position themselves as leaders in the new era of finance, delivering unparalleled value to their clients and organizations. The journey starts here, with a commitment to learning, exploring, and innovating with AI.

Chapter 2: Getting Started with AI Tools

Chapter 2: Getting Started with AI Tools

Artificial Intelligence (AI) is no longer a futuristic concept; it is a practical tool reshaping industries, including accounting. For accountants, understanding and leveraging AI can lead to significant improvements in efficiency, accuracy, and decision-making. However, diving into the world of AI can feel overwhelming, especially for those unfamiliar with its applications. This chapter aims to demystify AI by providing a clear, actionable guide to selecting, setting up, and using AI tools effectively in your accounting practice. By the end of this chapter, you will have a solid foundation to confidently integrate AI into your workflows.

Understanding AI Tools and Their Relevance to Accounting

To begin, it's essential to understand what AI tools are and how they can benefit accountants. AI encompasses a range of technologies, including machine learning, natural language processing (NLP), and automation, all of which can be applied to accounting tasks. Machine learning, for instance, enables systems to learn from data and improve over time without explicit programming. NLP allows AI to understand and process human language, making it useful for tasks like parsing contracts or generating reports. Automation, on the other hand, streamlines repetitive tasks such as data entry or invoice processing.

In accounting, AI tools can transform how you handle data, conduct analysis, and ensure compliance. For example, AI-powered software can automatically categorize expenses, flag anomalies in financial statements, or even predict cash flow trends based on historical data. These capabilities not only save time but also reduce the risk of human error, allowing accountants to focus on higher-value tasks like strategic planning and client advisory.

To fully appreciate the potential of AI in accounting, it's important to align these tools with your specific needs. Are you looking to automate routine tasks? Improve financial forecasting? Enhance compliance checks? Identifying your goals will help you choose the right AI tools and maximize their impact.

Criteria for Selecting the Right AI Tools

With a clear understanding of AI's relevance, the next step is selecting the right tools for your accounting practice. Not all AI tools are created equal, and choosing the wrong one can lead to inefficiencies or frustration. To make an informed decision, consider the following criteria:

Cost: AI tools can vary widely in price, from affordable SaaS solutions to expensive enterprise platforms. Determine your budget and ensure the tool provides a strong return on investment.

Ease of Use: As someone new to AI, you'll want a tool that is intuitive and user-friendly. Look for software with a clean interface, clear documentation, and accessible customer support.

Integration Capabilities: Your AI tool should seamlessly integrate with your existing accounting software and workflows. Check whether the tool supports APIs or plugins for popular platforms like QuickBooks, Xero, or Excel.

Scalability: As your practice grows, your AI tool should be able to scale with you. Consider whether the software can handle increased data volumes or additional users without compromising performance.

Support Services: Implementing AI can come with challenges, so robust support is crucial. Look for providers that offer training resources, troubleshooting assistance, and regular updates.

Creating a checklist based on these criteria can simplify the selection process and ensure you choose a tool that aligns with your firm's needs and goals.

Step-by-Step Guide to Setting Up AI Software

Once you've selected the right AI tool, the next challenge is setting it up effectively. This process can feel daunting, but breaking it down into manageable steps can make it more approachable.

Start by familiarizing yourself with the software's interface and features. Most AI tools offer tutorials or onboarding guides to help users get started. Dedicate time to exploring these resources before diving into the setup.

Next, configure the tool to align with your accounting workflows. This may involve importing existing data, setting up automation rules, or customizing reporting templates. Take care to ensure accuracy during this step, as errors in configuration can lead to incorrect outputs.

Training is another critical component of the setup process. Ensure your team understands how to use the tool and its key functionalities. Consider scheduling a training session or creating a shared resource, such as a user manual or video tutorial, to support ongoing learning.

Finally, anticipate potential challenges and have a plan in place to address them. For instance, if the tool encounters an error or produces unexpected results, know how to troubleshoot or seek support from the provider. By preparing for these scenarios, you can minimize disruptions and ensure a smooth transition to using AI in your practice.

Exploring Basic AI Functionalities in Accounting

With your AI tool set up, it's time to explore its basic functionalities and how they can benefit your accounting practice. While specific features will vary depending on the software, most AI tools offer the following capabilities:

Automation of Repetitive Tasks: AI can handle time-consuming, repetitive tasks like data entry, invoice processing, or bank reconciliation. For example, instead of manually categorizing expenses, an AI tool can automatically classify transactions based on predefined rules, saving hours of work.

Predictive Financial Insights: Many AI tools use machine learning to analyze historical data and generate predictive insights. These predictions can help you forecast cash flow, identify trends, or assess the financial health of a client's business.

Error Detection and Compliance: AI can scan financial data for anomalies or inconsistencies, flagging potential errors or compliance issues. This functionality is particularly valuable for ensuring accuracy in financial statements or adhering to regulatory requirements.

Real-world examples can bring these functionalities to life. Consider a scenario where an accountant uses an AI tool to automate invoice processing. By uploading invoices directly to the software, the AI extracts relevant data, categorizes expenses, and updates the accounting system in real time. This not only reduces manual effort but also minimizes the risk of errors, leading to more accurate financial records.

To leverage these functionalities effectively, experiment with different features and explore how they can enhance your workflows. Don't hesitate to reach out to the tool's support team for guidance or inspiration on how others in your industry are using the software.

Common Pitfalls and How to Avoid Them

While AI offers numerous benefits, it's important to be aware of common pitfalls and how to avoid them. One frequent mistake is underestimating the time and effort required for training. Implementing AI is not a one-time task; it requires ongoing learning and adaptation. Ensure you allocate sufficient resources for training and support to maximize the tool's value.

Another pitfall is over-reliance on automation. While AI can handle many tasks, it's not infallible. Always review outputs for accuracy and maintain a human oversight component, especially for critical processes like financial reporting or audits.

Data privacy is another concern when using AI tools. Ensure the software complies with relevant regulations, such as GDPR or HIPAA, and implement safeguards to protect sensitive information. This may include encrypting data, limiting access to authorized users, or conducting regular security audits.

By anticipating these challenges and taking proactive measures, you can avoid costly mistakes and ensure a successful AI integration.

Integrating AI into your accounting practice may seem like a daunting task, but with the right approach, it can significantly enhance your efficiency, accuracy, and value to clients. This chapter has provided a comprehensive guide to selecting, setting up, and using AI tools effectively. By understanding the relevance of AI to accounting, carefully selecting the right tools, and exploring their functionalities, you can unlock the full potential of this transformative technology.

Remember, adopting AI is a journey, not a destination. Start small, focus on your most pressing needs, and gradually expand your use of AI as you gain confidence and expertise. The insights and practical tips in this chapter will serve as a valuable resource as you embark on this journey, helping you navigate the challenges and seize the opportunities that AI offers. Embrace the future of accounting, and let AI empower you to achieve greater success in your profession.

Chapter 3: Automating Routine Tasks

Introduction: The Role of AI in Routine Accounting Tasks

In the ever-evolving world of finance, accountants are often burdened with repetitive, time-consuming tasks that, while essential, can detract from more strategic and value-driven activities. Artificial intelligence (AI) offers a transformative solution to this challenge, enabling accountants to automate routine processes, reduce errors, and enhance efficiency. This chapter explores how AI can revolutionize three key areas of accounting: data entry automation, invoice processing, and payroll management. By leveraging AI tools, accountants can not only streamline their workflows but also focus on higher-level responsibilities that drive business success.

The benefits of AI-driven automation are manifold. First, it significantly reduces the time spent on repetitive tasks, allowing accountants to allocate their expertise to more complex and insightful work. Second, AI minimizes human error, ensuring greater accuracy in financial data processing. Third, automation enhances compliance by ensuring that tasks are performed consistently and in accordance with regulatory requirements. As we delve into each of these areas, we'll provide practical advice on selecting the right AI solutions, integrating them into existing workflows, and avoiding common pitfalls. Real-world case studies will illustrate the transformative impact of AI in accounting practices, offering inspiration and guidance for your own journey toward automation.

Data Entry Automation: Streamlining Repetitive Tasks

Data entry is one of the most labor-intensive tasks in accounting, often requiring hours of manual effort to input financial data into systems. However, with AI-driven tools, this process can be streamlined significantly. Technologies such as Optical Character Recognition (OCR) and Natural Language Processing (NLP) have made it possible to automatically extract and input data from various sources, including invoices, receipts, and bank statements.

OCR technology scans physical or digital documents and converts the text into machine-readable data. This eliminates the need for manual data entry and reduces the risk of errors. For example, an AI-powered OCR tool can extract data from a supplier invoice, such as the invoice number, date, and total amount, and automatically input it into your accounting software. NLP enhances this process by interpreting the context of the data, ensuring that it is categorized correctly and matched with the appropriate accounts.

When selecting an AI tool for data entry automation, consider its compatibility with your existing systems. Look for solutions that integrate seamlessly with your accounting software, ensuring a smooth transition and minimizing disruptions to your workflow. Additionally, prioritize tools that offer robust data validation features to ensure accuracy. For instance, some AI tools can cross-reference extracted data with previous records to identify discrepancies and flag potential errors.

Real-world examples highlight the transformative impact of data entry automation. One accounting firm implemented an AI-powered OCR tool to process client receipts and invoices. Previously, this task required hours of manual effort, but with automation, the firm reduced processing time by 70% and significantly improved accuracy. This allowed the firm's accountants to focus on more strategic tasks, such as financial analysis and client advisory services.

Invoice Processing: Enhancing Accuracy and Efficiency

Invoice processing is another area where AI can deliver substantial benefits. Traditionally, this process involves multiple steps, from receiving invoices and verifying details to matching them with purchase orders and issuing payments. Each of these steps is prone to delays and errors, especially when handled manually. AI-powered solutions can automate the entire invoice processing workflow, enhancing accuracy and efficiency.

AI tools can automatically capture invoice data using OCR and NLP technologies, eliminating the need for manual data entry. They can then match the invoice details with corresponding purchase orders and flag any discrepancies for review. For example, if the invoice amount differs from the purchase order, the AI tool can alert the accountant to investigate the issue. This not only reduces errors but also ensures timely payments, improving vendor relationships.

Implementing AI-driven invoice processing requires careful planning. Start by evaluating your current workflow to identify pain points and areas for improvement. Choose an AI solution that integrates with your accounting and procurement systems, ensuring seamless data flow between platforms. Additionally, ensure that the tool offers robust reporting features, allowing you to track invoice statuses and identify bottlenecks in the process.

A case study from a mid-sized manufacturing company illustrates the benefits of AI-powered invoice processing. The company implemented an AI tool that automated the entire invoice workflow, from capture to payment. As a result, the company reduced invoice processing time by 50% and minimized errors, ensuring accurate and timely payments. This allowed the accounting team to focus on strategic tasks, such as cost optimization and financial planning.

Payroll Management: Simplifying Complex Processes

Payroll management is a complex and critical function in accounting, involving tasks such as calculating salaries, deducting taxes, and generating reports. Errors in payroll can lead to compliance issues and employee dissatisfaction, making accuracy paramount. AI offers a solution by automating these tasks and ensuring compliance with ever-changing payroll regulations.

AI-powered payroll software can automatically calculate salaries based on employee hours, deduct taxes, and generate pay slips. It can also handle complex payroll scenarios, such as overtime, bonuses, and deductions, ensuring accurate calculations. Additionally, AI tools can stay updated with the latest tax laws and regulations, reducing the risk of non-compliance. For example, some AI tools can automatically adjust payroll calculations when tax rates change, ensuring that your organization remains compliant.

When selecting AI payroll software, prioritize solutions that integrate with your HR and accounting systems. This ensures seamless data flow and minimizes manual intervention. Additionally, ensure that the software offers robust security features to protect sensitive employee data. Look for tools that provide real-time reporting and analytics, enabling you to monitor payroll expenses and identify trends.

A real-world example showcases the impact of AI on payroll management. A retail chain implemented AI-powered payroll software to automate salary calculations and tax deductions. Previously, the payroll process required significant manual effort and was prone to errors. With automation, the company reduced payroll processing time by 60% and ensured compliance with tax regulations. This allowed the accounting team to focus on strategic initiatives, such as optimizing labor costs and improving employee benefits.

Avoiding Common Pitfalls in AI Implementation

While AI offers significant benefits, its implementation can pose challenges. One common issue is data privacy concerns, especially when handling sensitive financial information. To address this, ensure that your AI solutions comply with data protection regulations and implement robust security measures. Conduct regular audits to verify data accuracy and security.

Integration with existing systems is another potential hurdle. To mitigate this, choose AI tools that offer seamless integration with your accounting software and other platforms. Work closely with vendors to ensure a smooth transition and provide training for your staff to familiarize them with the new system.

Resistance to change can also hinder AI adoption. To overcome this, emphasize the benefits of automation, such as reduced workload and improved accuracy. Involve your team in the implementation process and provide ongoing support to address any concerns.

A case study from a financial services firm highlights the importance of proper planning and training in AI implementation. The firm faced initial resistance from its accounting team when introducing AI-powered data entry tools. However, by involving the team in the selection process and providing comprehensive training, the firm successfully overcame resistance and achieved significant efficiency gains.

Embracing AI for a More Efficient Future

Artificial intelligence is transforming the accounting profession, enabling accountants to automate routine tasks and focus on strategic, high-value activities. By leveraging AI tools for data entry automation, invoice processing, and payroll management, you can enhance efficiency, reduce errors, and ensure compliance. However, successful implementation requires careful planning, proper integration, and ongoing evaluation.

As you embark on your AI journey, remember that the goal is not to replace human expertise but to augment it. Embrace AI as a tool that empowers you to deliver greater value to your clients and organization. Explore AI solutions tailored to your needs, stay informed about emerging technologies, and continuously refine your workflows to maximize the benefits of automation. By doing so, you'll position yourself and your organization for a more efficient and competitive future in the evolving world of finance.

Chapter 4: AI for Financial Analysis

AI for Financial Analysis

The world of accounting is undergoing a profound transformation, driven by the rapid advancements in artificial intelligence (AI). Financial analysis, once a labor-intensive process reliant on manual data entry and spreadsheet calculations, is now being revolutionized by AI-powered tools that enhance accuracy, efficiency, and strategic decision-making. For accountants, understanding how to harness these technologies is no longer optional—it's a necessity to remain competitive in an increasingly data-driven profession.

This chapter explores the role of AI in financial analysis, focusing on predictive analytics, trend analysis, and risk assessment. We'll begin by breaking down the fundamentals of AI-driven financial analysis, then examine real-world applications, advanced strategies, and common pitfalls to avoid. By the end, you'll have a clear roadmap for integrating AI into your financial workflows, empowering you to deliver deeper insights and greater value to your clients or organization.

Fundamentals of AI-Driven Financial Analysis

At its core, AI-driven financial analysis leverages machine learning (ML), natural language processing (NLP), and predictive modeling to automate and enhance traditional accounting tasks. These technologies enable accountants to move beyond reactive reporting and into proactive, data-driven decision-making.

Machine learning algorithms excel at identifying patterns in large datasets, making them ideal for tasks like forecasting and anomaly detection. For example, an ML model can analyze years of financial data to predict future revenue trends with far greater accuracy than manual extrapolation. Similarly,

NLP allows AI systems to parse unstructured data—such as earnings reports or news articles—to extract relevant financial insights, reducing the time accountants spend on manual research.

Predictive modeling, another key component, uses historical data to forecast future outcomes. This is particularly valuable for budgeting and cash flow projections, where even small errors can have significant consequences. AI-powered tools can continuously refine their predictions as new data becomes available, ensuring that forecasts remain accurate and up-to-date.

The benefits of AI in financial analysis are clear: increased accuracy, reduced manual effort, and the ability to scale operations without proportional increases in labor. Leading accounting firms and finance departments are already using platforms like IBM Watson, Microsoft Azure AI, and specialized fintech solutions to automate routine tasks and uncover hidden insights.

Practical Applications of AI in Financial Analysis

AI is not just a theoretical concept—it's already being applied in tangible ways across the accounting profession. One of the most impactful applications is automated financial forecasting. Traditional forecasting methods often rely on static models that struggle to account for market volatility or unexpected disruptions. AI, however, can dynamically adjust forecasts based on real-time data, providing accountants with a more reliable foundation for strategic planning.

Trend analysis is another area where AI shines. By analyzing vast amounts of transactional and market data, AI tools can identify emerging trends that might otherwise go unnoticed. For instance, an AI system might detect a gradual shift in consumer spending behavior before it becomes apparent in quarterly reports, allowing businesses to adjust their strategies proactively.

Risk assessment has also been transformed by AI. In investment portfolios, machine learning models can evaluate the risk profiles of various assets, flagging potential red flags or opportunities based on historical performance and market conditions. Similarly, AI-powered compliance tools can scan financial records for irregularities, reducing the risk of regulatory penalties and fraud.

For accountants looking to integrate AI into their workflows, the key is to start with specific, high-impact use cases. Automated expense categorization, real-time financial dashboards, and fraud detection systems are all accessible entry points that deliver immediate value. Many cloud-based accounting platforms, such as QuickBooks and Xero, now offer AI-powered features that can be easily adopted without extensive technical expertise.

Advanced Strategies for Leveraging AI

Once accountants are comfortable with basic AI applications, they can explore more advanced strategies to unlock deeper insights. One powerful technique is using AI to optimize pricing strategies. By analyzing customer behavior, competitor pricing, and market conditions, AI models can recommend optimal price points that maximize profitability while remaining competitive.

Cash flow prediction is another area where AI excels. Traditional cash flow models often rely on linear projections, which can be inaccurate in volatile markets. AI, however, can incorporate a wide range of variables—from seasonal trends to macroeconomic indicators—to generate more nuanced and reliable predictions. This enables businesses to better manage working capital and avoid liquidity crises.

AI can also enhance strategic decision-making by providing actionable insights from complex datasets. For example, a retail company might use AI to analyze sales data across multiple locations, identifying underperforming stores and recommending targeted interventions. Similarly, a manufacturing firm could use AI to optimize inventory levels, reducing carrying costs without risking stockouts.

Case studies illustrate the transformative potential of these strategies. A mid-sized accounting firm, for instance, implemented an AI-driven audit tool that reduced the time spent on manual data review by 40%, allowing auditors to focus on higher-value analysis. Another example is a financial services company that used AI to automate its risk assessment process, resulting in a 30% reduction in loan defaults.

Avoiding Common Pitfalls and Mistakes

While the benefits of AI are substantial, adoption is not without challenges. One of the most common pitfalls is poor data quality. AI models are only as good as the data they're trained on, so accountants must ensure that their datasets are clean, complete, and representative. Implementing robust data governance practices is essential to avoid "garbage in, garbage out" scenarios.

Integration complexities can also pose a hurdle. Many accounting teams rely on legacy systems that weren't designed to work with modern AI tools. Overcoming this may require incremental upgrades or the use of middleware solutions that bridge the gap between old and new technologies.

Resistance to change is another barrier. Some accountants may be hesitant to adopt AI, fearing job displacement or a steep learning curve. Addressing these concerns requires clear communication about AI's role as a tool to augment—not replace—human expertise. Training programs and hands-on workshops can help teams build confidence in using AI effectively.

Ethical considerations must also be taken into account. AI systems can inadvertently perpetuate biases present in historical data, leading to unfair outcomes in areas like credit scoring or hiring. Accountants should work closely with data scientists to ensure that AI models are transparent, auditable, and aligned with ethical standards.

To successfully integrate AI, accountants should follow a structured roadmap: start small with pilot projects, invest in training, and gradually scale up as confidence grows. Continuous learning is critical, as AI technologies evolve rapidly. Staying informed about the latest developments through industry publications, webinars, and professional networks will ensure that accountants remain at the forefront of this transformation.

AI is reshaping financial analysis, offering accountants unprecedented opportunities to enhance accuracy, efficiency, and strategic insight. From predictive analytics to risk assessment, these technologies are not just futuristic concepts—they're practical tools that are already delivering real-world value.

By understanding the fundamentals, exploring practical applications, and adopting advanced strategies, accountants can position themselves as indispensable advisors in an AI-driven financial landscape. While challenges exist, they are surmountable with careful planning and a commitment to continuous learning.

The future of accounting belongs to those who embrace AI as a partner in innovation. As you move forward, remember that the goal is not to replace human judgment but to empower it with deeper, data-driven insights. The journey may require adaptation, but the rewards—greater efficiency, sharper foresight, and a competitive edge—are well worth the effort.

Chapter 5: Enhancing Audit Processes with AI

Chapter 5: Enhancing Audit Processes with AI

The audit process has long been a cornerstone of financial integrity, but the rise of artificial intelligence (AI) is transforming how accountants approach this critical function. AI is no longer a futuristic concept—it's a practical tool that can automate tedious tasks, enhance accuracy, and uncover insights that might otherwise go unnoticed. For accountants looking to stay ahead, understanding how AI can be applied to auditing is essential. This chapter explores the key applications of AI in auditing, from fraud detection to compliance automation, and provides actionable insights for integrating these technologies into your workflow.

The Fundamentals of AI in Auditing

Before diving into specific applications, it's important to understand the foundational technologies driving AI in auditing. Machine learning (ML) and natural language processing (NLP) are two of the most relevant AI tools for accountants. ML algorithms analyze vast datasets to identify patterns, while NLP helps interpret unstructured data, such as contracts or emails, making it easier to extract relevant audit evidence.

One of the most immediate benefits of AI in auditing is automation. Tasks like data entry, reconciliation, and even preliminary risk assessments can now be handled by AI, freeing up auditors to focus on higher-value activities such as strategic analysis and client consultation. For example, AI-powered software can scan thousands of transactions in seconds, flagging inconsistencies that would take hours to identify manually.

However, adopting AI requires a basic familiarity with its terminology and capabilities. Terms like "supervised learning" (where AI is trained on labeled data) and "unsupervised learning" (where AI identifies patterns without predefined labels) may seem technical, but they simply describe how AI learns from data. The key for accountants is not to become AI experts overnight but to understand how these tools can complement their expertise.

AI-Powered Fraud Detection

Fraud detection is one of the most compelling applications of AI in auditing. Traditional methods often rely on random sampling or rule-based checks, which can miss sophisticated fraud schemes. AI, on the other hand, uses predictive analytics and anomaly detection to scrutinize every transaction, identifying irregularities that might indicate fraudulent activity.

For instance, AI can detect duplicate invoices, unusual payment patterns, or transactions that deviate from a company's typical behavior. A real-world example comes from a major retail firm that used AI to uncover a long-running vendor fraud scheme. The AI system flagged inconsistencies in invoice amounts and payment timing, which human auditors had overlooked due to the volume of data.

Another powerful feature of AI in fraud detection is its ability to learn over time. As the system processes more data, it becomes better at distinguishing between legitimate anomalies (like seasonal spikes in expenses) and potential red flags. This continuous improvement makes AI an invaluable ally in the fight against financial fraud.

Streamlining Compliance Checks with AI

Compliance is a growing challenge for businesses, with ever-evolving regulations like GDPR and SOX requiring meticulous record-keeping and reporting. AI can automate much of this burden by continuously monitoring transactions and flagging non-compliant activities in real time.

For example, AI tools can scan expense reports to ensure

they adhere to company policies or regulatory requirements. If an employee submits a receipt that violates travel policies, the system can flag it immediately, reducing the need for manual reviews. Similarly, AI can track changes in regulatory frameworks and automatically update compliance protocols, ensuring that audits remain aligned with the latest standards.

A case study from the banking sector illustrates this well. A mid-sized bank implemented AI to monitor transactions for anti-money laundering (AML) compliance. The system reduced false positives by 40%, allowing compliance officers to focus on genuinely suspicious activities rather than sifting through irrelevant alerts.

Automating Audit Trails

Audit trails are essential for transparency and accountability, but maintaining them manually is time-consuming and prone to errors. AI can automate this process by logging every action in a financial system, creating an immutable record that auditors can easily trace.

Blockchain technology, often paired with AI, enhances this capability further. For example, a blockchain-based audit trail ensures that once a transaction is recorded, it cannot be altered without leaving a trace. AI can then analyze these trails to detect inconsistencies or unauthorized changes, providing an additional layer of security.

A practical application of this is in inventory audits. AI-driven systems can track inventory movements in real time, automatically updating audit trails and flagging discrepancies. This not only saves time but also reduces the risk of human error in manual record-keeping.

Overcoming Challenges in AI Adoption

Despite its benefits, integrating AI into auditing is not without challenges. Data privacy concerns, resistance to change, and the need for upskilling are common hurdles. Here are some strategies to address them:

First, selecting the right AI tools is crucial. Look for solutions that integrate seamlessly with your existing systems and offer robust data security features. Pilot programs can help test the technology on a small scale before full implementation.

Second, invest in training. Accountants don't need to become data scientists, but a basic understanding of AI capabilities and limitations will foster confidence in using these tools. Many vendors offer training programs tailored to non-technical users.

Finally, ethical considerations must be front and center. Ensure that AI systems are transparent and free from bias, particularly in fraud detection and compliance, where false positives can have serious consequences.

AI is revolutionizing the audit process, offering unprecedented efficiency, accuracy, and insight. From detecting fraud to automating compliance checks and audit trails, these technologies empower accountants to focus on strategic decision-making rather than manual tasks. While challenges exist, they can be overcome with careful planning, training, and a commitment to ethical AI use.

For accountants willing to embrace this transformation, AI is not just a tool—it's a competitive advantage. By integrating AI into your audit processes, you can enhance your firm's capabilities, reduce risk, and deliver greater value to clients. The future of auditing is here, and it's powered by AI.

Chapter 6: AI in Tax Preparation and Planning

AI in Tax Preparation and Planning

Artificial Intelligence (AI) is revolutionizing industries across the globe, and the field of taxation is no exception. For accountants, the integration of AI into tax preparation and planning offers unprecedented opportunities to enhance accuracy, efficiency, and client value. This chapter explores the transformative role of AI in taxation, providing a comprehensive guide to its applications, benefits, and practical implementation. Whether you are new to AI or seeking to deepen your understanding, this chapter will equip you with the knowledge to leverage AI effectively in your practice.

Understanding AI-Driven Tax Code Analysis

One of the most complex aspects of tax preparation is navigating the labyrinth of tax codes and regulations. Traditional methods of interpretation are time-consuming and prone to human error. Enter AI-driven tax code analysis, a game-changer in decoding and understanding intricate tax laws. At the heart of this technology is Natural Language Processing (NLP), a branch of AI that enables machines to comprehend and analyze human language.

NLP algorithms can parse through thousands of pages of tax regulations, identifying relevant sections, updates, and compliance requirements with remarkable speed and accuracy. For example, an AI tool can scan a new tax bill, highlight changes that impact your clients, and flag potential compliance issues. This not only reduces the manual effort involved in tax code analysis but also ensures that accountants stay ahead of regulatory changes.

Consider the case of a mid-sized accounting firm that implemented an AI-driven tax code analysis tool. Previously, the firm relied on a team of experts to manually review and interpret tax regulations, a process that took weeks. With AI, the firm reduced this time to mere hours, allowing them to focus on strategic tax planning and client advisory services. Such examples underscore the transformative potential of AI in simplifying complex tax codes and enhancing compliance.

Advanced Tax Optimization with AI

Beyond code analysis, AI empowers accountants to move from reactive to proactive tax planning through advanced optimization strategies. Predictive analytics, a cornerstone of AI, allows accountants to forecast tax liabilities based on historical data, current financials, and future projections. By leveraging machine learning algorithms, accountants can identify trends, anticipate tax implications, and develop strategies to minimize liabilities.

Scenario modeling is another powerful tool enabled by AI. Accountants can create multiple tax scenarios for their clients, simulating the impact of different financial decisions. For instance, an AI system can model the tax consequences of investing in a new business venture versus expanding an existing one. This allows clients to make informed decisions that align with their financial goals while optimizing their tax positions.

A practical example of AI-driven tax optimization is seen in the case of a multinational corporation that used predictive analytics to manage its global tax liabilities. By analyzing data from various jurisdictions, the AI system identified opportunities for tax savings through optimized transfer pricing and strategic investments. The result was a significant reduction in the corporation's overall tax burden, coupled with enhanced compliance across multiple regions.

Automating Tax Filing Processes

Tax filing is often a labor-intensive process, fraught with the risk of errors and delays. AI-driven automation is transforming this critical function, streamlining data entry, error detection, and compliance checks. Automated tax filing systems can extract relevant data from financial records, populate tax forms, and perform real-time checks to ensure accuracy and compliance. This not only reduces the time spent on filing but also minimizes the risk of costly errors.

Popular AI-based tax software solutions, such as TurboTax and H&R Block, have already made significant strides in automating tax filing processes. These tools use machine learning algorithms to guide users through the filing process, flagging potential issues and suggesting deductions or credits. For accountants, adopting such tools can free up valuable time to focus on higher-value activities, such as client advisory and strategic planning.

Consider the example of a small accounting firm that transitioned to an AI-based tax filing system. The firm was able to reduce its filing time by 40%, while also improving accuracy and compliance. Clients benefited from faster turnaround times and fewer errors, enhancing their overall satisfaction. This case highlights the tangible benefits of automating tax filing processes with AI.

Real-World Applications and Case Studies

To fully appreciate the potential of AI in taxation, it is essential to examine real-world applications and case studies. One notable example is the use of AI by a mid-sized accounting firm to enhance its tax preparation services. The firm implemented an AI-driven tax code analysis tool, which enabled them to interpret complex regulations more efficiently and stay updated with changes. This not only improved compliance but also positioned the firm as a trusted advisor in the eyes of its clients.

Another compelling case is that of a multinational corporation that leveraged AI for tax optimization. By using predictive analytics and scenario modeling, the corporation was able to identify opportunities for tax savings across its global operations. The AI system provided actionable insights that informed strategic decisions, resulting in significant reductions in tax liabilities and enhanced compliance.

These real-world examples underscore the transformative impact of AI in taxation. By adopting AI-driven tools, accountants and firms can unlock new levels of efficiency, accuracy, and value-added services. However, it is equally important to navigate the challenges and pitfalls associated with AI adoption.

Overcoming Challenges and Avoiding Pitfalls

While the benefits of AI in taxation are clear, it is not without its challenges. Data privacy and security are paramount concerns, especially when dealing with sensitive financial information. Accountants must ensure that AI tools comply with data protection regulations and implement robust security measures to safeguard client data.

System integration is another challenge that accountants may face when adopting AI. Integrating AI tools with existing systems and workflows requires careful planning and execution. It is essential to choose AI solutions that are compatible with your current infrastructure and provide adequate training to your team.

Maintaining ethical standards is also critical when using AI in taxation. Accountants must ensure that AI-driven recommendations and decisions align with professional ethics and regulatory requirements. Transparency in AI algorithms and decision-making processes is key to building trust with clients and regulators.

Staying updated with evolving AI technologies and regulations is another challenge that accountants must navigate. The field of AI is rapidly advancing, and it is essential to keep abreast of new developments and best practices. Continuous learning and professional development are crucial for leveraging AI effectively in taxation.

AI is reshaping the landscape of tax preparation and planning, offering accountants powerful tools to enhance accuracy, efficiency, and client value. From AI-driven tax code analysis to advanced optimization strategies and automated filing systems, the applications of AI in taxation are vast and transformative. Real-world case studies demonstrate the tangible benefits of AI adoption, while also highlighting the challenges and pitfalls that must be navigated.

As AI continues to evolve, it is essential for accountants to stay informed and embrace these technologies with a strategic mindset. By integrating AI into their practice, accountants can not only streamline their workflows but also provide proactive, value-added services that position them as trusted advisors in an increasingly competitive landscape. The journey to mastering AI in taxation may present challenges, but the rewards are well worth the effort. Embrace the future of tax preparation and planning with AI, and unlock new possibilities for your practice and your clients.

Chapter 7: Integrating AI with Existing Systems

Integrating AI with Existing Systems

The integration of artificial intelligence into accounting workflows presents immense opportunities for efficiency, accuracy, and strategic decision-making. However, the process of merging AI with existing systems—particularly enterprise resource planning (ERP) platforms—requires careful planning and execution. This chapter provides a roadmap for accountants looking to harness AI without disrupting their current operations. We will explore compatibility considerations, data migration strategies, synchronization techniques, and real-world case studies to illustrate successful implementations. By the end of this chapter, you will have the knowledge to navigate AI integration confidently while avoiding common pitfalls.

Understanding AI Compatibility with ERP Systems

Before introducing AI tools, it is essential to assess how they will interact with your existing ERP system. Compatibility hinges on several technical factors, including application programming interfaces (APIs), data formats, and system architecture. APIs act as bridges between different software applications, allowing them to communicate seamlessly. When evaluating AI solutions, ask vendors whether their tools support API integration with your ERP system. If not, middleware—software that facilitates communication between incompatible systems—may be necessary.

Data formats are another critical consideration. AI tools often require structured data, while legacy ERP systems may store information in proprietary formats. Accountants should work with IT teams to ensure data can be extracted, transformed, and loaded (ETL) into a format the AI can process. For example, if your ERP system outputs reports in PDF format but the AI tool requires CSV files, automated conversion tools may be needed.

System architecture also plays a role. Cloud-based AI solutions may integrate more smoothly with modern, cloud-hosted ERPs, whereas on-premise AI tools might be better suited for traditional systems. A phased implementation approach—starting with a pilot project—can help identify compatibility issues before full-scale deployment.

Data Migration Strategies for AI Integration

Migrating data to an AI-enabled system is a delicate process that demands attention to detail. Poorly executed migrations can lead to data corruption, loss, or security vulnerabilities. The first step is data cleaning, which involves identifying and correcting errors, removing duplicates, and standardizing formats. For instance, inconsistent date formats (MM/DD/YYYY vs. DD/MM/YYYY) can cause significant issues in AI-driven forecasting models.

Next, consider the volume and sensitivity of the data being transferred. Large datasets may require batch processing to avoid system overload, while sensitive financial information must be encrypted during transit. Tools like Talend or Informatica can automate much of this process, reducing manual errors.

A critical but often overlooked aspect is data mapping—ensuring fields in the legacy system correctly correspond to those in the new AI environment. For example, if your ERP system uses "VendorID" but the AI tool expects "SupplierCode," mismatches can disrupt operations. Creating a detailed data dictionary before migration minimizes such risks.

Finally, validate the migrated data through reconciliation reports. Compare totals, sample records, and run test analyses to confirm accuracy. A well-executed migration sets the foundation for AI to deliver reliable insights.

Synchronizing AI with Legacy Systems

Many accounting departments rely on legacy systems that were not designed with AI in mind. Synchronizing these older platforms with modern AI tools requires creative solutions. One approach is adopting hybrid systems, where certain functions are handled by AI while others remain in the legacy environment. For example, an AI tool could manage invoice processing while the ERP system continues to handle general ledger entries.

Middleware solutions can also bridge the gap. These intermediary programs translate data between incompatible systems in real time, ensuring seamless operation. However, middleware adds complexity, so it is crucial to monitor performance and troubleshoot issues promptly.

Regular audits of synchronization processes help maintain compatibility. Schedule periodic checks to verify that data flows correctly between systems and that AI-generated outputs align with legacy system records. Proactive monitoring prevents small discrepancies from escalating into major problems.

Case Studies: Successful AI Integration in Accounting

Real-world examples illustrate the transformative potential of AI when integrated thoughtfully. One mid-sized accounting firm struggled with manual expense reporting, a time-consuming process prone to errors. By implementing an AI-powered expense management tool that integrated with their existing ERP system, they reduced processing time by 60% and virtually eliminated data entry mistakes. The key to their success was a thorough compatibility assessment and a phased rollout that allowed for adjustments based on user feedback.

Another case involves a manufacturing company that used AI to enhance its accounts payable workflow. The AI tool automatically matched purchase orders, invoices, and delivery receipts, flagging discrepancies for human review. This integration required custom middleware to connect the AI solution with their decades-old ERP system, but the investment paid off in reduced processing costs and improved vendor relationships.

These examples highlight the importance of aligning AI capabilities with organizational needs and existing infrastructure.

Avoiding Common Pitfalls in AI Integration

Even with careful planning, challenges can arise. One frequent mistake is underestimating the importance of data quality. AI tools are only as good as the data they process, and incomplete or inaccurate datasets lead to unreliable outputs. Invest time in data cleaning and validation before integration.

Another pitfall is failing to train staff adequately. Accountants and finance professionals must understand how to interpret AI-generated insights and troubleshoot basic issues. Provide hands-on training sessions and create reference materials to support the transition.

Finally, avoid over-customization. While tailoring AI tools to specific needs is tempting, excessive modifications can make future updates difficult. Strike a balance between customization and maintaining the software's core functionality.

Integrating AI into accounting systems is not without its challenges, but the rewards—increased efficiency, reduced errors, and deeper financial insights—make the effort worthwhile. By ensuring compatibility with ERP systems, executing careful data migrations, and synchronizing with legacy platforms, accountants can harness AI's full potential. The case studies and pitfalls discussed in this chapter provide a practical foundation for successful implementation. With thoughtful planning and a commitment to continuous improvement, AI can become an invaluable ally in modern accounting.

Chapter 8: Advanced AI Strategies for Accountants

Advanced AI Strategies for Accountants

The accounting profession is undergoing a profound transformation, driven by the rapid evolution of artificial intelligence. While many accountants have begun to explore basic AI tools, mastering advanced applications can unlock unprecedented efficiency, accuracy, and strategic value. This chapter delves into the sophisticated AI strategies reshaping financial workflows, from machine learning models to AI-driven forecasting and custom solutions. By understanding these technologies, accountants can elevate their practice, mitigate risks, and position themselves as forward-thinking leaders in the field.

Understanding Machine Learning Models in Accounting

Machine learning (ML) is the backbone of many AI applications in accounting. At its core, ML enables systems to learn from data, identify patterns, and make predictions without explicit programming. For accountants, this means automating complex tasks, uncovering hidden insights, and improving decision-making.

There are three primary types of machine learning models: supervised, unsupervised, and reinforcement learning. Supervised learning relies on labeled data to train algorithms for specific outcomes, such as fraud detection or invoice classification. For example, an ML model can be trained on historical transaction data to flag suspicious activities with high accuracy. Unsupervised learning, on the other hand, identifies patterns in unlabeled data, making it ideal for anomaly detection or clustering similar financial behaviors. Reinforcement learning, though less common in accounting, involves systems learning through trial and error, which could optimize processes like tax planning over time.

Practical applications of ML in accounting are vast. Fraud detection algorithms can analyze millions of transactions in seconds, reducing the risk of financial loss. Predictive analytics can forecast cash flow trends, enabling proactive financial planning. Even routine tasks like expense categorization can be automated with ML, freeing accountants to focus on higher-value advisory roles.

To integrate ML into accounting workflows, start by identifying repetitive or data-intensive tasks. Partner with data scientists to select the right algorithms and ensure high-quality data inputs. Pilot small-scale projects to test effectiveness before scaling up. The key is to view ML not as a replacement for human expertise but as a powerful tool that enhances accuracy and efficiency.

Harnessing AI-Driven Forecasting for Financial Planning

Financial forecasting has long been a cornerstone of accounting, but traditional methods often fall short in today's volatile markets. AI-driven forecasting leverages advanced algorithms to analyze vast datasets, detect subtle trends, and generate more accurate predictions.

Time series analysis is a foundational technique for financial forecasting. By examining historical data points over time, AI models can identify seasonal patterns, cyclical trends, and irregularities. For instance, a retail company might use time series analysis to predict holiday sales spikes and adjust inventory accordingly. Regression models, another powerful tool, assess relationships between variables—such as how changes in interest rates impact revenue—to refine financial projections.

Neural networks, inspired by the human brain, take forecasting a step further by processing complex, nonlinear relationships in data. These models excel at handling multifaceted scenarios, such as predicting stock performance based on macroeconomic indicators, company financials, and even sentiment analysis from news articles.

A compelling case study involves a mid-sized manufacturing firm that implemented AI-driven forecasting to overhaul its budgeting process. By integrating neural networks with historical sales data, market trends, and supplier lead times, the firm reduced forecasting errors by 30% and improved its working capital management. The AI system flagged potential cash flow shortfalls months in advance, allowing the finance team to secure favorable financing terms.

To adopt AI-driven forecasting, begin by consolidating clean, structured data from multiple sources. Collaborate with IT or data specialists to select the right model for your needs. Start with short-term forecasts to build confidence before tackling long-term projections. Most importantly, use AI outputs as a complement to human judgment, not a replacement—context and intuition remain critical in financial decision-making.

Building Custom AI Solutions for Unique Accounting Needs

While off-the-shelf AI tools offer valuable capabilities, custom solutions can address the unique challenges faced by individual firms or clients. Developing tailored AI applications requires a strategic approach, from problem identification to implementation.

The first step is pinpointing specific pain points. For example, a tax advisory firm might struggle with efficiently analyzing client portfolios for optimization opportunities. A custom AI solution could automate the extraction of relevant data from tax returns, investment statements, and regulatory updates, flagging potential savings or risks.

Selecting the right algorithms is next. Decision trees might suffice for straightforward classification tasks, while deep learning models could be necessary for parsing unstructured data like contracts or emails. Collaboration with data scientists is essential here—they can translate accounting requirements into technical specifications and ensure the solution aligns with business goals.

Real-world examples highlight the potential of custom AI. One accounting firm developed a proprietary tool to audit expense reports across multinational clients. The AI system cross-referenced receipts, travel logs, and company policies, reducing audit time by 50% and improving compliance. Another firm created a chatbot to handle routine client queries about tax deadlines or document submissions, freeing staff to focus on complex cases.

The development process should be iterative. Start with a minimum viable product (MVP), gather feedback, and refine the solution. Ensure robust testing to avoid errors that could have financial or reputational consequences. Custom AI is an investment, but the long-term gains in efficiency, accuracy, and client satisfaction often justify the effort.

Avoiding Common Pitfalls in AI Adoption

Despite its potential, AI adoption in accounting is not without challenges. Recognizing and mitigating these risks is crucial for a successful transition.

One of the most common pitfalls is inadequate data quality. AI models are only as good as the data they're trained on. Incomplete, inconsistent, or biased data can lead to flawed outputs. To address this, establish rigorous data governance practices. Cleanse existing datasets, standardize formats, and implement ongoing data quality checks.

Another challenge is the lack of in-house expertise. Many accounting firms lack the technical skills to develop or manage AI solutions. Bridging this gap may require upskilling staff through training programs or partnering with external experts. Encourage a culture of continuous learning to keep pace with AI advancements.

Resistance to change is another barrier. Accountants accustomed to traditional methods may view AI as a threat rather than a tool. To overcome this, demonstrate AI's value through small wins—such as automating a tedious task—and involve teams in the implementation process. Highlight how AI can enhance their roles by eliminating drudgery and enabling more strategic work.

Finally, ethical considerations cannot be overlooked. AI systems must comply with regulations like GDPR and ensure transparency in decision-making. Avoid over-reliance on black-box models where outputs are inexplicable. Prioritize fairness, accountability, and client trust in every AI application.

The integration of advanced AI strategies into accounting is no longer a futuristic concept—it's a present-day imperative. Machine learning models are revolutionizing fraud detection and predictive analytics, while AI-driven forecasting is delivering unprecedented accuracy in financial planning. Custom AI solutions offer tailored answers to unique challenges, and by sidestepping common pitfalls, firms can ensure smooth adoption.

For accountants, the path forward involves embracing AI as a collaborative partner. The profession's future lies not in resisting technological change but in harnessing it to deliver deeper insights, greater efficiency, and enhanced client value. By mastering these advanced strategies, accountants can secure their relevance in an increasingly AI-driven world. The tools are here; the opportunity is now.

Chapter 9: Case Studies: AI Success Stories

Introduction to AI Success Stories in Accounting

Artificial intelligence (AI) is transforming industries across the globe, and accounting is no exception. For accountants, AI offers a unique opportunity to enhance efficiency, accuracy, and strategic decision-making. However, understanding how to effectively integrate AI into accounting practices can feel daunting, especially for professionals who are not yet familiar with its applications. This chapter aims to bridge that gap by presenting real-world case studies that demonstrate the successful implementation of AI in accounting and finance.

These case studies are carefully selected to illustrate the practical applications of AI in accounting, highlighting the challenges faced, the solutions applied, and the measurable outcomes achieved. By examining these success stories, accountants can gain valuable insights into how AI can be leveraged to automate routine tasks, improve financial forecasting, and detect fraudulent activities. Moreover, these examples serve as a roadmap for professionals looking to adopt AI in their own practices, providing actionable advice and lessons learned from those who have already navigated this journey.

The transformative potential of AI in accounting lies in its ability to process vast amounts of data quickly and accurately, identify patterns, and generate actionable insights. However, the key to successful AI adoption lies in understanding how to apply these capabilities effectively within the unique context of accounting. This chapter explores this process through detailed case studies, offering a comprehensive guide for accountants ready to embrace AI.

Case Study 1: Automating Accounts Payable with AI

One of the most common challenges in accounting is the manual processing of accounts payable (AP), which can be time-consuming, error-prone, and costly. A mid-sized accounting firm faced these very issues when dealing with a high volume of invoices. Their manual AP process involved extensive data entry, which led to frequent errors and delays in payment processing. To address these challenges, the firm decided to implement AI-driven solutions, specifically optical character recognition (OCR) and machine learning (ML) algorithms.

OCR technology was used to automatically extract data from invoices, eliminating the need for manual data entry. This not only reduced errors but also significantly sped up the process. The firm then applied ML algorithms to categorize invoices, match them with purchase orders, and flag discrepancies. Over time, the system learned from past transactions, improving its accuracy and efficiency.

The results were remarkable. The firm reported a 60% reduction in processing time and a 50% decrease in data entry errors. Additionally, the automation of AP tasks allowed staff to focus on more strategic activities, such as vendor relationship management and financial analysis. This case study demonstrates how AI can transform mundane, repetitive tasks into streamlined, efficient processes, freeing up valuable time and resources.

Case Study 2: Enhancing Financial Forecasting with Predictive Analytics

Financial forecasting is a critical aspect of accounting, yet it often relies on historical data and assumptions that may not reflect future realities. A large corporation sought to improve the accuracy of its financial forecasts by leveraging AI-powered predictive analytics. The company faced challenges in accurately predicting revenue trends, which impacted its ability to allocate resources effectively and make informed strategic decisions.

To address these challenges, the corporation implemented AI tools such as time-series analysis and neural networks. Time-series analysis allowed the company to identify patterns in historical data, while neural networks provided the ability to model complex relationships between variables. These tools enabled the corporation to generate more accurate forecasts by incorporating a broader range of data points and identifying subtle trends that traditional methods might overlook.

The implementation of predictive analytics had a profound impact on the corporation's decision-making process. Forecast accuracy improved by 30%, leading to better resource allocation and more informed strategic planning. Additionally, the ability to anticipate revenue trends allowed the company to proactively address potential challenges, such as cash flow shortages or market fluctuations. This case study highlights the power of AI in enhancing financial forecasting and its potential to drive more effective decision-making.

Case Study 3: Fraud Detection Using AI Algorithms

Fraud detection is a critical concern for financial services companies, where even a single fraudulent transaction can have significant repercussions. A financial services company sought to enhance its fraud detection capabilities by deploying AI algorithms. The company faced challenges in identifying fraudulent transactions in real-time, as traditional rule-based systems often flagged legitimate transactions as suspicious, leading to false positives.

To address this issue, the company implemented anomaly detection techniques and supervised learning models. Anomaly detection allowed the system to identify unusual patterns in transaction data, while supervised learning models were trained on historical data to recognize fraudulent behavior. The AI system continuously learned from new data, improving its ability to detect genuine fraud while reducing false positives.

The results were impressive. The company achieved a 40%

improvement in fraud detection accuracy and a 25% reduction in false positives. Additionally, the AI system enabled real-time monitoring of transactions, allowing the company to respond to potential fraud more quickly and effectively. This case study underscores the importance of continuous learning and adaptation in maintaining an effective fraud detection system and highlights the potential of AI to enhance security in financial services.

Lessons Learned and Best Practices

The case studies presented in this chapter offer valuable lessons for accountants looking to adopt AI in their practices. One of the key takeaways is the importance of selecting the right AI tools for specific tasks. For example, OCR and ML algorithms were highly effective in automating accounts payable, while predictive analytics proved invaluable in enhancing financial forecasting. Understanding the unique capabilities of different AI tools is essential for successful implementation.

Another critical lesson is the need to manage implementation challenges effectively. AI adoption often requires significant investment in technology, training, and change management. Accountants must be prepared to address these challenges by building a strong business case, securing buy-in from stakeholders, and fostering a culture of innovation within their organizations.

Finally, continuous learning and adaptation are essential for maximizing the benefits of AI. As demonstrated in the fraud detection case study, AI systems must be continuously updated with new data to maintain their accuracy and effectiveness. Accountants should prioritize ongoing training and development to ensure they remain at the forefront of AI advancements.

Key Takeaways and Next Steps

The case studies in this chapter illustrate the transformative potential of AI in accounting, offering practical examples of how AI can streamline processes, enhance accuracy, and drive strategic decision-making. For accountants ready to embark on their AI journey, the lessons learned from these success stories provide valuable guidance.

To begin, accountants should evaluate their current processes and identify areas where AI can add the most value. Building a business case for AI adoption is essential, as it helps secure the necessary resources and support from stakeholders. Additionally, accountants should invest in training and development to build their AI expertise and foster a culture of innovation within their organizations.

For those seeking further learning, a wealth of resources is available, including online courses, industry publications, and professional networks. By leveraging these resources and applying the lessons learned from the case studies discussed in this chapter, accountants can successfully integrate AI into their practices and unlock its full potential.

In conclusion, AI is no longer a futuristic concept; it is a practical tool that can revolutionize accounting practices. By learning from real-world success stories and adopting best practices, accountants can navigate the complexities of AI adoption and position themselves at the forefront of innovation in their profession.

Chapter 10: Avoiding Common AI Pitfalls

Avoiding Common AI Pitfalls

As artificial intelligence (AI) continues to reshape the accounting profession, its potential to streamline workflows, enhance accuracy, and unlock new insights is undeniable. However, like any transformative technology, AI comes with its own set of challenges. Understanding and navigating these pitfalls is essential for accountants to maximize the benefits of AI while minimizing risks. This chapter explores the most common obstacles encountered when implementing AI in accounting, offering practical strategies to address them effectively. By focusing on data privacy concerns, avoiding over-reliance on AI systems, navigating implementation mistakes, and building a resilient AI strategy, accountants can ensure a smooth and successful integration of AI into their practice.

Understanding Data Privacy Concerns in AI

Data privacy is a cornerstone of trust in the accounting profession, and it becomes even more critical when leveraging AI systems. AI relies heavily on large datasets to function effectively, and much of this data is sensitive, including client financial records, tax information, and personal identifiers. The risks of data breaches, unauthorized access, and non-compliance with regulations like the General Data Protection Regulation (GDPR) are significant concerns.

One of the first steps in safeguarding data privacy is selecting AI tools with robust security features. Look for systems that offer end-to-end encryption, multi-factor authentication, and regular security updates. Additionally, implementing data access controls ensures that only authorized personnel can interact with sensitive information. For example, role-based access systems can limit data exposure to only those who need it for their specific tasks.

Real-world examples underscore the importance of data privacy. In 2020, a major accounting firm experienced a data breach due to inadequate encryption of client files stored in an AI-driven platform. The incident not only resulted in financial losses but also damaged the firm's reputation. Lessons from such cases highlight the necessity of proactive measures, such as conducting regular security audits and ensuring compliance with data protection regulations.

Finally, fostering a culture of data privacy within your organization is essential. Educate your team about the risks and best practices, and encourage a mindset where data protection is everyone's responsibility.

While AI can automate repetitive tasks and enhance decision-making, over-reliance on AI systems can lead to significant drawbacks. AI is not infallible; it can make errors, particularly in nuanced or complex scenarios that require human judgment. For instance, AI may struggle to interpret ambiguous financial data or understand the context behind certain transactions.

To mitigate this risk, it's crucial to maintain a balance between AI automation and human oversight. One effective strategy is to implement regular audits of AI-generated outputs. These audits can identify errors or inconsistencies that require human intervention. Additionally, continuous training for your team ensures they remain proficient in interpreting AI results and making informed decisions.

Another approach is fostering collaboration between AI systems and accounting professionals. Encourage your team to view AI as a tool that complements their expertise rather than replaces it. For example, AI can handle data entry and preliminary analysis, while accountants focus on strategic insights and client communication. This collaborative mindset not only enhances accuracy but also leverages the unique strengths of both AI and human professionals.

Real-world examples illustrate the dangers of over-reliance. In one case, an accounting firm automated its entire payroll process using AI, only to discover recurring errors in employee tax withholdings. The oversight caused significant financial penalties and eroded client trust. By incorporating human oversight from the start, such pitfalls can be avoided.

Navigating Common Implementation Mistakes

Implementing AI systems is a complex process that requires careful planning and execution. Common mistakes include inadequate preparation, lack of user training, and mismatched expectations. For example, some organizations rush into AI adoption without clearly defining their goals or understanding the technology's capabilities, leading to suboptimal outcomes.

A successful AI implementation begins with goal setting. Identify specific challenges you aim to address with AI, such as improving audit efficiency or enhancing fraud detection. Next, secure stakeholder buy-in by communicating the benefits and potential ROI of AI adoption. Involve your team early in the process to address concerns and build enthusiasm.

Pilot testing is another critical step. Start with a small-scale implementation to evaluate the system's performance and identify any issues. Use feedback from the pilot phase to refine the system before full deployment. Additionally, invest in comprehensive training for your team to ensure they are comfortable using the new technology.

Case studies of successful AI implementations provide valuable insights. For instance, a mid-sized accounting firm successfully integrated AI for real-time financial analysis by following a phased approach. They began with training sessions for their staff, followed by a pilot test in one department, and gradually expanded the system firmwide. This methodical approach minimized disruptions and maximized the benefits of AI.

Building a Resilient AI Strategy

As AI technology evolves, so must your strategy for leveraging it. Building a resilient AI strategy involves staying updated with advancements, fostering a culture of innovation, and regularly reviewing AI systems to ensure they align with organizational goals.

Start by staying informed about the latest developments in AI. Attend industry conferences, participate in webinars, and collaborate with AI vendors to understand emerging trends and tools. This knowledge can help you identify opportunities to enhance your accounting practice and stay ahead of competitors.

Fostering a culture of innovation is equally important. Encourage your team to experiment with AI tools and share their insights. Create a safe environment where they can propose new ideas and learn from failures. This mindset not only drives progress but also ensures your organization remains adaptable in a rapidly changing landscape.

Regularly reviewing your AI systems is essential to maintain their effectiveness. Conduct periodic assessments to evaluate whether the technology is meeting your objectives and identify areas for improvement. For example, if your AI system is no longer providing accurate forecasts, it may be time to update the underlying algorithms or retrain the model with new data.

Finally, invest in continuous learning for your team. Provide opportunities for them to acquire new skills in AI and data analytics. This investment not only enhances their expertise but also ensures your organization is well-equipped to harness the full potential of AI.

The integration of AI into accounting practices offers immense opportunities to enhance efficiency, accuracy, and decision-making. However, it also comes with challenges that require careful navigation. By addressing data privacy concerns, avoiding over-reliance on AI systems, navigating common implementation mistakes, and building a resilient AI strategy, accountants can harness the full potential of AI while maintaining compliance, accuracy, and professional integrity.

As you embark on your AI journey, remember that success lies in balancing technology with human expertise. AI is a powerful tool, but it is not a substitute for the judgment, creativity, and empathy that define the accounting profession. With a thoughtful and strategic approach, you can unlock the transformative benefits of AI and position your practice for long-term success in an increasingly digital world.

Chapter 11: Actionable Advice for Immediate Implementation

Chapter 11: Actionable Advice for Immediate Implementation

Artificial intelligence is no longer a futuristic concept—it's a present-day tool reshaping the accounting profession. For accountants looking to stay competitive, integrating AI into daily workflows is no longer optional; it's essential. This chapter provides a clear, practical roadmap to help you implement AI solutions immediately, even if you're just starting your journey with this technology. We'll begin with foundational concepts, explore quick wins for fast results, and guide you through step-by-step implementation. By the end, you'll have the knowledge and confidence to harness AI's power in your accounting practice.

Understanding the Basics of AI for Accountants

Before diving into implementation, it's crucial to grasp the core AI technologies relevant to accounting. Machine learning, natural language processing (NLP), and automation are the pillars of AI-driven accounting solutions. Machine learning enables systems to learn from data patterns, improving accuracy over time—ideal for tasks like fraud detection or financial forecasting. NLP allows AI to interpret and generate human-like text, streamlining client communications or parsing contracts. Automation reduces manual effort in repetitive tasks such as data entry or reconciliation.

A common misconception is that AI will replace accountants. In reality, AI augments human expertise by handling tedious, time-consuming tasks, freeing professionals to focus on strategic analysis and client relationships. For example, AI can process thousands of transactions in seconds, flagging anomalies for your review, but it's your judgment that determines the next steps.

Quick Wins: Leveraging AI for Immediate Results

The best way to build confidence with AI is to start with quick wins—simple, high-impact applications that deliver visible benefits. Here are three areas where AI can make an immediate difference:

Invoice Processing: Manual invoice entry is error-prone and time-consuming. AI-powered tools like Dext or Bill.com extract data from invoices automatically, categorize expenses, and sync them with your accounting software. To get started, upload a batch of invoices to the platform, allow the AI to process them, and review the results for accuracy. Most tools improve over time as they learn your preferences.

Expense Tracking: AI-driven apps such as Expensify or Rydoo automate expense reporting by scanning receipts, extracting relevant details, and populating expense reports. Employees simply snap photos of receipts, and the AI handles the rest. This reduces administrative overhead and ensures compliance with company policies.

Anomaly Detection: AI excels at identifying irregularities in financial data. Tools like MindBridge Ai Auditor analyze transactions for unusual patterns, flagging potential fraud or errors. Set up the tool to monitor key accounts, configure alert thresholds, and review flagged items regularly. Even basic implementations can significantly reduce risk.

These quick wins require minimal setup but deliver tangible efficiency gains. They also serve as a foundation for more advanced AI adoption.

Step-by-Step Implementation Guide

Once you've experimented with quick wins, it's time to develop a structured AI integration plan. Follow these steps to ensure a smooth transition:

Assess Your Needs: Identify pain points where AI can add the most value. Are you struggling with month-end close delays? Spending too much time on data entry? Prioritize solutions that address these challenges.

Select the Right Tools: Research AI-powered accounting software that aligns with your needs. Look for platforms with strong user reviews, robust support, and scalability. Popular options include Xero (for small businesses), BlackLine (for automation), and Workiva (for compliance).

Train Your Team: Successful AI adoption depends on user buy-in. Organize training sessions to familiarize your team with new tools. Highlight how AI will simplify their workflows rather than replace their roles. Many vendors offer free webinars or onboarding support.

Set Measurable Goals: Define what success looks like. For example, aim to reduce invoice processing time by 50% or cut manual reconciliation efforts by 30%. Track progress and adjust your approach as needed.

Start Small, Scale Gradually: Begin with a pilot project—such as automating expense tracking for one department—before rolling it out company-wide. This minimizes disruption and allows for fine-tuning.

Best Practices for Long-Term Success

AI is not a one-time implementation; it requires ongoing attention to deliver sustained value. Follow these best practices to maximize your investment:

Prioritize Data Quality: AI's output is only as good as its input. Ensure your financial data is clean, consistent, and well-organized. Regularly audit data sources to eliminate duplicates or errors.

Monitor Performance: Review AI-generated reports and alerts to verify accuracy. If the system flags too many false positives, adjust its sensitivity settings. Continuous feedback improves AI precision.

Stay Updated: AI technology evolves rapidly. Subscribe to industry newsletters, attend webinars, and participate in forums to stay informed about new features or tools.

Avoid Over-Reliance: AI is a powerful assistant, but human oversight remains critical. Always validate AI recommendations, especially for high-stakes decisions like compliance or financial forecasting.

Real-World Case Studies and Insights

To illustrate AI's transformative potential, consider these real-world examples:

Streamlined Audits: A mid-sized accounting firm implemented MindBridge Ai Auditor to analyze 100% of client transactions instead of relying on random sampling. The AI identified several material misstatements that traditional methods missed, enhancing audit quality and client trust.

Enhanced Forecasting: A corporate finance team used an AI-powered forecasting tool like Planful to analyze historical data and market trends. The AI generated predictive models that improved budget accuracy by 20%, enabling better strategic decisions.

Improved Client Services: A tax advisory firm integrated NLP-based chatbots to handle routine client queries about deductions or filing deadlines. This freed up staff to focus on complex tax planning, boosting client satisfaction and retention.

These cases demonstrate how AI can drive efficiency, accuracy, and competitive advantage—outcomes within reach for any accounting professional willing to embrace the technology.

AI is reshaping accounting, and the time to act is now. By starting with quick wins, following a structured implementation plan, and adhering to best practices, you can seamlessly integrate AI into your workflows. Remember, AI isn't about replacing accountants—it's about empowering you to work smarter, faster, and with greater insight. The tools and strategies outlined in this chapter provide a clear path to immediate benefits and long-term success. Take the first step today, and position yourself at the forefront of the AI-driven future of accounting.

Chapter 12: The Future of AI in Accounting

Chapter 12: The Future of AI in Accounting

The accounting profession stands at the cusp of a transformative era, driven by the rapid evolution of Artificial Intelligence (AI). As AI technologies become increasingly sophisticated, they are reshaping the way accountants work, offering unprecedented opportunities for efficiency, accuracy, and innovation. Yet, this shift also brings challenges, from ethical considerations to the need for new skills and competencies. This chapter explores the future of AI in accounting, focusing on emerging trends, long-term impacts, and practical strategies for accountants to adapt and thrive in an AI-driven world.

Emerging Trends in AI and Accounting

AI is already making waves in accounting, and its influence is only set to grow. One of the most significant trends is the use of machine learning algorithms for predictive analytics. These algorithms analyze vast amounts of historical financial data to forecast future trends, enabling accountants to make more informed decisions. For instance, predictive analytics can help businesses anticipate cash flow issues, identify potential risks, and optimize investment strategies.

Natural Language Processing (NLP) is another game-changing technology. NLP allows AI systems to understand and generate human language, making it possible to automate report generation, draft financial summaries, and even respond to client queries. This not only saves time but also enhances the clarity and accessibility of financial information.

Robotic Process Automation (RPA) is revolutionizing repetitive tasks such as data entry, invoice processing, and reconciliation. By automating these mundane activities, accountants can focus on higher-value tasks like strategic planning and client advisory services. Furthermore, AI-powered audit tools are enhancing the accuracy and efficiency of audits, while blockchain technology is being integrated to improve transparency and security in financial transactions.

These emerging trends are not just about automating tasks—they are about augmenting human capabilities. AI is enabling accountants to deliver deeper insights, more accurate forecasts, and better strategic guidance, ultimately adding greater value to their clients and organizations.

Long-Term Impacts on the Accounting Profession

As AI becomes more pervasive, its long-term impacts on the accounting profession will be profound. One of the most discussed implications is job displacement. While AI can automate many routine tasks, it is unlikely to replace the need for skilled accountants entirely. Instead, the role of accountants will evolve, with a greater emphasis on strategic advisory, ethical oversight, and complex problem-solving.

Ethical considerations will also come to the forefront. As AI systems handle sensitive financial data, issues of data privacy and algorithmic bias will need to be addressed. Accountants will play a critical role in ensuring that AI technologies are used responsibly and transparently. Additionally, the profession will need to grapple with questions of fairness and accountability, particularly when AI systems are involved in decision-making processes.

Another long-term impact is the need for reskilling and upskilling. As AI takes over routine tasks, accountants will need to develop new competencies, such as data analysis, AI system management, and ethical oversight. Soft skills like critical thinking, emotional intelligence, and adaptability will also become increasingly important. By embracing lifelong learning, accountants can position themselves as indispensable partners in an AI-driven world.

It is crucial to view AI not as a competitor but as a collaborator. AI can augment human expertise, enabling accountants to deliver more value and insights than ever before. By understanding and embracing these long-term impacts, accountants can proactively adapt to the changing landscape and secure their place in the future of the profession.

Preparing for an AI-Driven Future

To thrive in an AI-driven future, accountants must take proactive steps to integrate AI into their workflows and develop the necessary skills. One of the first steps is to invest in AI tools that align with your specific needs. Whether it's predictive analytics software, NLP-powered report generators, or RPA platforms, selecting the right technology can significantly enhance your efficiency and effectiveness.

Continuous education is essential. Many organizations offer courses and certifications in AI and related fields, providing accountants with the knowledge and skills they need to leverage these technologies. Engaging in professional development opportunities, attending industry conferences, and participating in AI-focused communities can also keep you informed about the latest trends and best practices.

Developing soft skills is equally important. As AI handles more routine tasks, accountants will need to focus on areas where human expertise excels, such as strategic planning, client communication, and ethical oversight. Skills like critical thinking, emotional intelligence, and adaptability will be invaluable in navigating the complexities of an AI-driven world.

Integration is key. Rather than viewing AI as a standalone tool, consider how it can enhance your existing processes. Collaborate with technology partners to ensure seamless implementation, and regularly evaluate the effectiveness of AI tools to make necessary adjustments. By adopting a strategic approach to AI integration, you can maximize its benefits and minimize potential disruptions.

Finally, create a roadmap for your AI journey. Identify your goals, assess your current capabilities, and outline the steps needed to achieve your objectives. Whether it's automating specific tasks, enhancing your data analysis capabilities, or improving client advisory services, having a clear plan will help you stay focused and motivated.

Case Studies: AI Success Stories in Accounting

Real-world examples illustrate the transformative power of AI in accounting. One notable case is the use of AI for fraud detection. By analyzing patterns in financial transactions, AI systems can identify anomalies that may indicate fraudulent activity. For example, a global accounting firm implemented an AI-powered fraud detection system, significantly reducing the time and effort required to identify and investigate potential fraud cases.

Tax optimization is another area where AI is making a difference. AI systems can analyze complex tax codes and regulations, identifying opportunities for savings and ensuring compliance. A mid-sized accounting firm leveraged AI to streamline its tax preparation process, resulting in faster turnaround times and improved client satisfaction.

Financial forecasting has also benefited from AI. Predictive analytics tools can analyze historical data and market trends to generate accurate forecasts, helping businesses make informed decisions. A corporate finance department used AI to improve its forecasting accuracy, enabling better strategic planning and resource allocation.

These success stories demonstrate the practical applications of AI in accounting, offering valuable insights and inspiration for accountants looking to embrace these technologies.

Avoiding Common Pitfalls

While AI offers immense potential, there are pitfalls to avoid. One common mistake is over-reliance on technology. AI is a powerful tool, but it is not infallible. Accountants must maintain a critical eye, verifying AI-generated insights and ensuring that human oversight is in place.

Inadequate data governance is another challenge. AI systems rely on high-quality data to function effectively. Poor data management practices, such as inconsistent data entry or incomplete records, can undermine the accuracy and reliability of AI tools. Establishing robust data governance protocols is essential to maximize the benefits of AI.

Resistance to change can also hinder AI adoption. Embracing AI requires a cultural shift, with a focus on innovation and continuous improvement. Accountants must be open to new ways of working and willing to invest time and resources in learning and integrating AI technologies.

To avoid these pitfalls, take a measured approach to AI adoption. Start with small projects, evaluate their effectiveness, and gradually scale up as you gain confidence and experience. Collaborate with experienced technology partners to ensure smooth implementation, and prioritize ongoing education to stay ahead of the curve.

Conclusion

The future of AI in accounting is both exciting and challenging. As AI technologies continue to evolve, they will transform the way accountants work, offering new opportunities for efficiency, accuracy, and innovation. However, this shift also requires accountants to adapt, developing new skills, embracing ethical considerations, and integrating AI into their workflows.

By staying informed about emerging trends, understanding the long-term impacts, and taking proactive steps to prepare, accountants can position themselves for success in an AI-driven world. The case studies and practical advice provided in this chapter offer a roadmap for embracing AI, enabling accountants to deliver greater value to their clients and organizations.

Ultimately, AI is not just a tool—it is a catalyst for growth and transformation. By embracing this technology, accountants can redefine their role, elevate their expertise, and shape the future of the profession. The journey ahead may be complex, but with the right mindset and strategies, the possibilities are limitless.

www.ingramcontent.com/pod-product-compliance
Lightning Source LLC
LaVergne TN
LVHW102013210926
848483LV00011B/378
* 9 7 8 1 9 1 4 2 7 2 6 9 1 *